May 15

Dear Diary,

   Today I had quite an adventure!
A hungry bird picked me up in its beak
to eat me. But it dropped me on the wet
soil. Now my hard shell is becoming soft.

Your Friend,

Sunny

This is me
in my shell.

May 17

Dear Diary,

   Big day! Today I started to germinate. That means I began to grow. My root is reaching way down into the wet soil to get water. Right now, water is all I need to grow.

Your Friend,

Sunny

My root

My root is covered with tiny hairs.

May 20

Dear Diary,

    S-T-R-E-T-C-H! My root is growing longer. Other smaller roots are growing off my big root. My shell is filled with good food that helps me grow.

Your Friend,

Sunny

Growing down!

May 22

Dear Diary,

Today, I pushed and pushed and finally popped out of the ground. There was plenty of sunshine to keep me warm. What a pretty world!

Your Friend,

Sunny

Pushing hard...

Almost there...

Hello, world!

Dear Diary,

I feel so grown up! I used up all the food in my shell. Now I have lovely green leaves. My leaves use the Sun to make food, so I can keep growing.

Your Friend,

Sunny

June 12

Dear Diary,

I am growing taller and taller! My leaves and stem turn towards the Sun to get light. At the same time, my roots keep stretching deep into the ground to get water. I'm a very busy plant!

Your Friend,

Sunny

Sometimes, I get water from a friend!

June 19

Dear Diary,

My stem is so strong. That's a good thing because it has to hold up my leaves. They are getting bigger and bigger. My stem also carries water and minerals from the ground to my leaves. It works like a giant straw!

Your Friend,

Sunny

June 23

Dear Diary,

Today a caterpillar munched a hole in one of my leaves. Ouch! That hurt! Luckily, a strong wind blew that caterpillar off my leaf before it could eat too much. Whew!

Your Friend,

Sunny

My leaf almost became a caterpillar's lunch!

July 17

Dear Diary,

Hooray! My bud is showing. It has a cover to protect it from insects and bad weather. Many tiny petals are growing inside my bud.

Your Friend,

Sunny

My bud

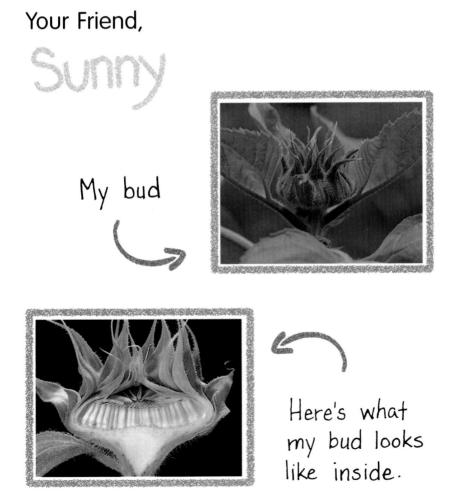

Here's what my bud looks like inside.

July 21

Dear Diary,

Look! My bud is opening up! Bright yellow petals are unfolding. The petals look like a golden crown. I am starting to look just like my name!

Your Friend,

Sunny

Dear Diary,

I have grown so much! I am taller than my friend. I am even taller than a grown-up person! I am reaching for the Sun.

Your Friend,

Sunny

July 31

Dear Diary,

   I feel great! I am in full bloom now.
My flower is as big as a beach ball.
Don't you think I'm beautiful?

Your Friend,
Sunny

August 1

Dear Diary,

I had a visitor today. A bee stopped by. It came to sip my nectar. It also brought me pollen from another sunflower. The pollen will help me make new seeds.

Your Friend,

Sunny

August 14

Dear Diary,

A lot has happened. Do you see how my flower is drooping? That's because I am making lots of seeds. They are very, very heavy!

Your Friend,

Sunny

August 15

Dear Diary,

I am full of ripe seeds! Some will become sunflowers like me. Others will become food for birds and people. My petals and leaves are beginning to die. But that's OK. My seeds are most important now.

Your Friend,

Sunny

My flower holds hundreds of seeds.

Dear Diary,

    I had a great life! I did a great job! My seeds will help people and animals. Best of all, new sunflowers will grow from them. Maybe they will keep a diary just like me!

Your Friend,

Sunny